ESSENTIAL LIBRARY OF
AMERICAN WARS

VIETNAM WAR

ABDO
Publishing Company

VIETNAM WAR

BY MARTIN GITLIN

CONTENT CONSULTANT

Kenneth Heineman
Professor and Chair, History Department, Angelo State University

CREDITS

Published by ABDO Publishing Company, PO Box 398166, Minneapolis, MN 55439. Copyright © 2014 by Abdo Consulting Group, Inc. International copyrights reserved in all countries. No part of this book may be reproduced in any form without written permission from the publisher. The Essential Library™ is a trademark and logo of ABDO Publishing Company.

Printed in the United States of America,
North Mankato, Minnesota
052013
012014

♻ THIS BOOK CONTAINS AT LEAST 10% RECYCLED MATERIALS.

Editor: Arnold Ringstad
Series Designer: Emily Love

Library of Congress Control Number: 2013932676

Cataloging-in-Publication Data
Gitlin, Martin.
 Vietnam War / Martin Gitlin.
   p. cm. -- (Essential library of American wars)
Includes bibliographical references and index.
ISBN 978-1-61783-880-4
1. Vietnam War, 1961-1975--History--Juvenile literature. 2. Vietnam War, 1961-1975--Vietnam--Juvenile literature.   I. Title.
959.704--dc23

                                                              2013932676

CONTENTS

1

SURPRISE ATTACK

By 1968, death and destruction had been a daily reality in Vietnam for decades. War had ravaged the small Southeast Asian nation since the end of World War II (1939–1945). But the guns were supposed to fall silent on January 31, 1968. South Vietnam, backed by the United States, and North Vietnam, backed by the Soviet Union and China, pledged to hold a ceasefire during Tet, the traditional Vietnamese New Year holiday.

US troops welcomed the planned peace. The bloody conflict had already taken the lives of more than a million people, including tens of thousands of Americans. The US forces were sent halfway around the world to fight alongside their South Vietnamese allies. The United States had been involved for several years in the battle against North Vietnam, which sought to unify the country under Communist rule. US troops contended not only with North Vietnam's organized

The expected calm of the Tet holiday soon gave way to an all-out battle.

military, but also with Communist guerrilla forces in South Vietnam known as the Vietcong.

There were hints on January 30 that the Communists were not planning to celebrate Tet peacefully. The Vietcong smuggled rifles underneath bunches of flowers into the South Vietnamese capital of Saigon. North Vietnamese soldiers dressed as South Vietnamese soldiers hitched rides on American transports.

The enemy's secret plan worked perfectly. US and South Vietnamese troops slept securely with the belief that the Tet holiday would bring a lull in hostilities. So when US soldier Alan Dawson woke to the pitter-patter of rubber sandals on his rooftop, he was surprised. He later learned the sounds were Communist soldiers preparing an attack on a Saigon police station.

Dawson survived what became known as the Tet Offensive, but US military policeman Charles L. Daniel was not as fortunate. Daniel was stationed in the US Embassy in Saigon. In the middle of the night, 19 armed men burst in and began shooting.

The Vietcong entered the grounds of the US Embassy through a hole they blew in its wall.

Associated Press journalist Peter Arnett was one of many US reporters covering the war when the Communists launched the Tet Offensive. But his fellow correspondents did not have their families with them at the time. Arnett did.

Arnett responded to the gunfire by herding his wife and two children into an apartment bathroom. He figured the thick walls made it the safest place for his family. He then raced to his office to cover the attack that would alter the course of the war.

"They're coming in, they're coming in!" he yelled into his radio to his superiors. "Help me! Help me!"[1] It was too late. Daniel was gunned down. Soon thousands of Vietcong guerrillas were leaving a path of death and devastation through the streets of Saigon.

US soldiers and civilians scrambled to stay alive. A group of missionaries ducked for cover in a garbage pit they had converted into a bunker. Among them were Robert Ziemer and Ed Thompson. Ziemer tried to surrender by raising his arms when enemy soldiers raced toward them, but he was killed. So was Thompson, who screamed out "Mercy, mercy," as he tried in vain to shield his wife from the hail of bullets.[2]

Marines rest after a battle in the besieged city of Hue in February 1968.

WRONG TIME, WRONG PLACES

US military leaders had anticipated a Communist offensive early that year, but certainly not one during the Tet holiday. Neither did they expect the offensive to be so widespread.

The anticipated target was Khe Sanh, a US base in the northwest corner of South Vietnam on which the enemy had already focused. But the extensive operation was not centered anywhere. The attack ranged across the entire country.

Among the bloodiest spots was the South Vietnamese city of Hue, where marines were pinned down by Communist troops for nearly a month before they could break free. In all, the Tet Offensive resulted in approximately 81,000 deaths, including 4,000 Americans, 5,000 South Vietnamese, an estimated 58,000 North Vietnamese and Vietcong, and 14,000 civilians.[3]

Yet despite the chaos it caused, the operation was a military failure for the Communists. Security soon returned to the US Embassy. South Vietnamese and US forces eventually drove out the enemy from other areas of the country. The Communist forces had hoped to convince the South Vietnamese people to join the fight against the Americans and drive them out of their country, but they failed to achieve this objective.

However, the Tet Offensive did succeed in one important way. It helped turn US public opinion against the war. Millions of people throughout the United States watched on television as horror unfolded in the streets of South Vietnam. Night after night, they watched Americans die on the news. They were horrified when they witnessed a South Vietnamese police chief execute a member of the Vietcong as the cameras rolled. "We knew the attack was going to have a psychological effect on the Americans," said former Vietcong guerrilla commander Tong Viet Duong. "We were told America was growing tired of the war."[4]

Though many Americans initially rallied to President Lyndon B. Johnson during the coordinated attack, public opinion in the United States began shifting against involvement in Vietnam. Many people saw no end in sight for the war. They did not believe preventing a Communist takeover in a small, faraway country was worth thousands of US lives.

POWERFUL ALLY TO THE ANTIWAR MOVEMENT

Civil rights leader Martin Luther King Jr. was concerned in the 1960s about ending racial discrimination in the United States. He was among the most influential black leaders in US history. He also had strong opinions against the Vietnam War.

On April 4, 1967, he gave a speech titled "Declaration of Independence from the War in Vietnam" at a New York church. He expressed his desire the war should end: "In order to atone for our sins and errors in Vietnam, we should take the initiative in bringing the war to a halt."[5] King was murdered on that same date one year later in Memphis, Tennessee.

General William Westmoreland was accused during and after the Vietnam War of giving false hope to political leaders and the US people. One piece of evidence was a speech he gave to the National Press Club just two months before the Tet Offensive in which he claimed the United States was on the verge of winning the war.

"We have reached an important point when the end begins to come into view," he said. "I am absolutely certain that, whereas in 1965 the enemy was winning, today he is certainly losing. The enemy's hopes are bankrupt."[6]

At the same time, many Americans did not want to see the United States defeated in Vietnam. Johnson and his successor would face major challenges in navigating the complexities of public opinion.

UNWARRANTED OPTIMISM?

Military leaders such as General William Westmoreland had been telling the US people for several years that their country was on the verge of winning the war. But the wide-ranging Communist attacks proved the enemy was still alive and well.

Protesters' criticisms of President Johnson became increasingly harsh as the war dragged on.

LOSING CRONKITE, LOSING THE COUNTRY

The most respected journalist in the country in 1968 was TV news anchorman Walter Cronkite. Cronkite broadcast from Vietnam during the Tet Offensive. When he returned to the United States, he offered his view that the best the country could hope for was a stalemate and thousands more deaths. He further stated the only honorable solution was to negotiate a peace settlement. His opinion about the Vietnam War carried a lot of weight among most Americans.

Before the Tet Offensive, polls showed more than half of Americans supported Johnson's war policy. That number plummeted in the wake of the attack. A myth grew that Johnson, upon seeing the broadcast, moaned, "If I've lost Cronkite, I've lost the country."[8] In reality, Johnson could not have watched the broadcast. He was in Texas helping celebrate the birthday of Governor John Connally. But there was a grain of truth in the story. Most Americans remained against the war for its duration.

The Tet Offensive intensified the antiwar movement in the United States. Millions participated in protest demonstrations on college campuses and in city streets. College students, aware people their own age were being killed daily in Vietnam, were especially vigilant. They believed the war to be a moral outrage. Perhaps the most memorable chant screamed out by protesters included the initials of the president's full name, Lyndon Baines Johnson: "Hey, hey, L. B. J., how many kids did you kill today?"[7]

Johnson grew increasingly upset by such criticism. He understood the cost of US involvement in Vietnam and knew the heated debates over the war were ripping the country apart. He was torn between his desire to pull out and his commitment to preventing a Communist takeover in South Vietnam. He believed in the domino theory, the idea that the fall of one country to Communism would lead to the fall of others.

Pressure to pull US troops from Vietnam threatened to sink Johnson's presidency. Threats even came from his own Democratic Party. Antiwar candidates Eugene McCarthy and Robert F. Kennedy were shaping up to be formidable foes for the 1968 Democratic presidential nomination.

Johnson stunned the nation on March 31, 1968, when he announced he would not seek a second term in office. He was dropping out of the race. Johnson told the nation he could not justify waging a campaign and a war at the same time. The new president would be forced to deal not just with a conflict in Vietnam, but also with angry Americans who wished their country had never gotten involved in the war.

THE ORIGINS OF THE WAR

In the centuries leading up to the 1900s, European nations established colonies in various parts of the world. In particular, the United Kingdom and France sought to expand their influence across the globe. They competed with each other to gain territory and exploit native peoples for their own benefit. However, differing colonization strategies led to vastly different results.

Generally, the United Kingdom tried to establish peace and the rule of law in the places it conquered. Keeping the peace also made it easier to profit financially from its colonies. France, however, tended to side with particular groups inside the countries it colonized. In many cases—most notably in Vietnam—this led to conflict. The French stirred discontent

In the 1880s, French colonial military forces clashed against Chinese troops to win control of what is now Vietnam.

and violence in Vietnam, leading to a civil war that would not end until 1975.

The first French foray into Vietnam began in the 1600s, when missionaries sought to bring Christianity to the Vietnamese people. In the 1800s, French military intervention unified the north and south areas of Vietnam into one nation. By 1893, France controlled what are now Vietnam, Laos, and Cambodia under the name French Indochina. Though local rulers were largely left in power, the French controlled all of them behind the scenes. The French and their puppet rulers oppressed the native people and destroyed all dissent. The colonizers worked only to profit from their colony and ignored the plight of its citizens. They sought to keep the Vietnamese people uneducated and poor.

Under such conditions, resistance seemed inevitable. Eventually, a man who called himself Ho Chi Minh, or "He Who Enlightens," launched an uprising. He was the son of a Vietnamese official who had resigned in protest of French rule. Ho worked from the 1920s to the early 1940s to organize groups dissatisfied with foreign control of their country into one force called the Vietminh.

Ho Chi Minh gives a public address in France.

His world travels as a young man had brought him to London, England, and Paris, France, where he helped create the French Communist Party. Yet despite his Communist ties, he maintained a friendship with the United States during World War II as the Vietminh worked with the Americans to defeat Japan. That relationship was destined to falter. The United States considered the Communist system a threat to democracy and grew wary of its spread anywhere in the world. By the end of World War II, the United States was the only combatant with a functioning economy. It emerged as the top power on the world stage. Along with this power came responsibility, as much of the world needed to be rebuilt and rehabilitated. US leaders sought to avoid the colonial conflicts faced by the British and the French. At the same time, they wanted to counter the expansion of the Communist Soviet Union's influence in the world. It was this desire that led to the United States supporting the French in their struggle against Ho Chi Minh.

In 1946, the First Indochina War (1946–1954) broke out as Vietminh forces attacked their French occupiers. For eight long years, the US-backed French battled the Communist Vietnamese forces supported by the Soviet Union and later by China, which had been taken over by Communists in 1949. A decisive battle in 1954 ended the conflict, though the peace it achieved would be short-lived.

BATTLE OF DIEN BIEN PHU

The end of French colonialism in Vietnam occurred in the town of Dien Bien Phu in 1954. There the Vietminh surrounded and routed a force of 12,000 French troops. France begged for help from the United States, but to no avail. Congress was not about to approve dispatching troops to Vietnam so soon after the United States had finished fighting the Korean War (1950–1953). That conflict had cost nearly 37,000 US lives.[1]

US President Dwight D. Eisenhower sought to solve the problem in Vietnam peacefully. Representatives of the United States, the Soviet Union, France, China, and other nations convened in 1954 in the neutral country of Switzerland. They emerged on July 21 with an agreement called the Geneva Accords granting Vietnam independence, though neither the United States nor South Vietnam formally accepted the terms of the

BOGGED DOWN IN KOREA

The US military had problems of its own in Asia while the French were attempting to maintain control of Vietnam. The United States fought the Korean War to prevent Communist control of Korea. The conflict represented the beginning of the United States' attempts to contain Communism in Asia, laying the groundwork for the Vietnam War.

The Korean War began when North Korea invaded South Korea and sought to impose a Communist government. The United States fought on the side of South Korea while China gave military assistance to North Korea. Though North Korea failed in its mission to unify Korea under Communist rule, it has maintained that system for itself and in the 2010s is considered one of the most repressive countries in the world.

agreement. The nation was divided into North Vietnam, led by Ho Chi Minh and the Vietminh, and South Vietnam, officially known as the Republic of Vietnam.

The plan was to unite the country in two years under one government based on fair and free elections. The United States was skeptical of the plan. US leaders dreaded the popularity of Ho Chi Minh would result in him winning the vote and establishing Communism throughout Vietnam.

However, the alternate leader left much to be desired. Brutal South Vietnamese leader Ngo Dinh Diem, originally installed by the Vietnamese

A CROOKED ELECTION

Vietnamese emperor Bao Dai named Ngo Dinh Diem as leader of South Vietnam following the Geneva Accords of 1954. But Bao Dai regretted the move and authorized a general to lead a coup that would overthrow Diem. It was a failure.

Diem called for an election against Bao Dai and made certain he would win. Diem supporters intimidated voters and fixed the balloting, and he won handily. Bao Dai returned to France, where he lived until his death in 1997. He outlived Diem by 34 years.

South Vietnam, which never signed the Geneva Accords, quickly disregarded the agreement and continued fighting the Communists.

emperor Bao Dai, refused to submit to the election process. He gave out high-level government jobs to his relatives. He also harshly persecuted Buddhists in his country, stealing land from them and giving it to fellow Catholics.

The US government was so fearful of a Communist takeover in Vietnam that it supported Diem anyway. He was invited to Washington, DC, to speak to both houses of Congress on May 9, 1957.

"We affirm that the sole legitimate object of the state is to protect the fundamental rights of human beings to existence—to the free development of their intellectual, moral, and spiritual life," he said.[3] Diem's

A DEFENSE OF DIEM

Diem convinced many in the US media that he was driven by religious freedom and equality. After his speech to Congress in 1957, the *New York Times* published an editorial praising Diem.

"This could have been expected from a man of deep religious heart," it read. "It is also not surprising that a firm concept of human rights should come from [an educated man]."[2] In truth, Diem had been oppressing the Buddhist population in his country since assuming control of South Vietnam.

Diem, *right*, met with Eisenhower, *left*, when he visited the United States in 1957.

speech sought to win over American public opinion, and media reports remarked on Diem's visit favorably.

SAYING ONE THING, DOING ANOTHER

Diem's words contradicted everything he represented to the people of South Vietnam. A group of citizens formed the National Liberation Front (NLF) to overthrow his rule. Some in that group went on to join the People's Liberation Armed Forces, the NLF's armed wing, also known as the Vietcong. The Vietcong killed thousands of Diem supporters. Some in the United States claimed the North Vietnamese were promoting revolution in South Vietnam. Others considered the backlash against Diem simply a natural reaction to his brutal leadership.

Both had valid points. The corrupt Diem government motivated a revolutionary spirit inside his country, which Ho encouraged. The North Vietnamese then gave military and economic support to the Vietcong, which gained enough strength to control some areas of South Vietnam by the late 1950s.

US officials grew more concerned by the year. Eisenhower's successor, John F. Kennedy, promised to prevent Communism from spreading, but he stopped short of sending combat troops

Helicopters would become critical tools for the US war effort in Vietnam.

to Vietnam upon taking office in 1961. He opted instead to dispatch thousands of military advisers to help train the Army of the Republic of Vietnam (ARVN) to defend their country. It was not an easy task. The growing hatred of Diem destroyed much of the soldiers' motivation to fight. Helicopter pilots arriving in December of that year were the first US troops involved in combat, but Kennedy never sent ground troops.

Uprisings against Diem became more frequent in the early 1960s. Buddhists protested their treatment under his rule. He tossed many of them and other political opponents in jail, where they were often tortured or killed. On June 11, 1963, one of the most famous protests in history took place at a

Duc's dramatic protest was later copied by a few American antiwar activists.

Saigon intersection. Buddhist monk Thich Quang Duc sat in a meditative position while another monk emptied a five-gallon (18.9 L) can of gasoline onto him. Duc then struck a match and dropped it on himself. He continued to sit still as he burned to death. Duc's protest against the persecutions carried out by the Diem regime was captured by photographers, and the grisly images brought worldwide attention to the struggle.

It was apparent to Kennedy and US military leaders that Diem was turning many South Vietnamese into Vietcong. The US Central Intelligence Agency backed a plan for the ARVN to overthrow Diem. With the United States giving assurances that it would not interfere in the coup, ARVN generals captured and killed Diem on November 2, 1963. After a series of short-lived military governments, Nguyen Van Thieu became the president of South Vietnam, a post he would hold from June 1965 until the country ceased to exist.

South Vietnam was in chaos after Diem's assassination. Kennedy considered his strategy options for Vietnam, but he was assassinated later that month, on November 22. Secretary of Defense Robert McNamara later expressed his belief that Kennedy would have withdrawn from Vietnam rather than get deeply involved in the war. But the course of US policy would now be directed by Kennedy's vice president and successor, Lyndon B. Johnson. The US presence and death toll would soon escalate dramatically.

GIVING THE GREEN LIGHT

President Johnson was torn. He did not want to get the nation bogged down in a war in Vietnam. But he also believed a Communist takeover was inevitable if US ground troops were not sent to aid the ARVN. He knew the United States had made a commitment to the South Vietnamese government to prevent such a takeover.

Johnson sent 7,000 more advisers to South Vietnam, raising the total to 23,000.[1] Still, he needed a provocation by the North Vietnamese to justify sending combat troops. He used what became known as the Gulf of Tonkin incident to increase US presence in Vietnam. On August 2, 1964, a North Vietnamese torpedo boat attacked a patrolling US warship, the USS *Maddox*. The attack was in response to a South

With the arrival of US advisers, the South Vietnamese military finally went on the offensive against the Vietcong.

Vietnamese naval attack two days earlier. On August 4, crews of the *Maddox* and the USS *Turner Joy* claimed they were under attack. Johnson retaliated by ordering air strikes against North Vietnamese targets. Yet no Americans were injured in either event. Most historians believe the events of August 4 were exaggerated or contrived to give Johnson an excuse to ask Congress for ground troops. Congress quickly and overwhelmingly passed the Gulf of Tonkin Resolution, allowing Johnson to take any steps he deemed necessary to prevent further aggression by North Vietnam.

DRAWING IN THE AMERICANS

The situation was becoming desperate for the South Vietnamese. The Vietcong controlled large portions of the country. Johnson believed for the first time Ho Chi Minh and the North Vietnamese Army (NVA) wanted to fight a war against the United States. The president felt his back was against the wall. "We have kept our guns over the mantel and our shells in the cupboard for a long time now," said Johnson. He later admitted he "suddenly realized that doing nothing was more dangerous than doing something."[2]

Each B-52 bomber aircraft could drop dozens
of 750-pound (340 kg) bombs.

Johnson ordered sustained bombing of North Vietnam in
March 1965 under the code name Operation Rolling Thunder.
It targeted military and industrial centers. It also targeted
the Ho Chi Minh trail, a network of roads and paths through
which weapons and soldiers from North Vietnam were being
transported to the Vietcong in the South.

The bombing failed to bring the desired results. Secretary of Defense Robert McNamara and General William Westmoreland asked for ground troops, and Johnson agreed. More than 70,000 were sent to Vietnam by the summer of 1965 and the total skyrocketed to 184,000 by the end of the year.[3] Their initial mission of defending air bases had expanded, and the soldiers were now tasked with tracking down and killing the Vietcong.

Most Americans supported Johnson's Vietnam policies. They were willing to give him time to win the war. Belief in the validity of the domino theory was widespread, and many wanted democracy brought to Southeast Asia. At the same time, opponents of that view pointed to the deposed Diem regime, arguing that South Vietnam was hardly a democracy.

Those who backed US involvement felt certain it would be a short war. They assumed US firepower and technology would overwhelm the relatively primitive enemy. After all, the United States had never lost a war. The nation had emerged from World War II as the most powerful in the world. Proponents of the war scoffed at the notion of North Vietnam and its Vietcong allies defeating the strongest military on Earth.

Author Philip Caputo expresses his feelings about arriving in Vietnam in his book *A Rumor of War*: "America seemed omnipotent then: the country could still claim it had never lost a war, and we believed we were ordained to play cops to the Communists' robber and spread our own political faith around the world."[4]

AN UNCONVENTIONAL WAR

The US military was fighting an unconventional war. There were no well-defined front lines. The enemy was nowhere to be seen but could seemingly appear from anywhere at any time. Gunfire rained down upon troops marching through mountains and jungles. Snipers and land mines killed or maimed US troops without warning. Soldiers were forced to seek out the enemy

A GROWING ANTIWAR MOVEMENT

The majority of Americans supported US policy in Vietnam early in the war, but the increase in troop strength and death tolls alarmed many. Activists, including many college students, grew increasingly angry and frustrated as young men were dispatched halfway around the world only to return in body bags. Students questioned the morality of US involvement.

Thousands began protesting on college campuses and in Washington, DC. One November 1965 demonstration in the nation's capital attracted an estimated 15,000 to 35,000 protesters.[5]

on search-and-destroy missions. They often could not distinguish between friendly South Vietnamese and the Vietcong.

The United States had been involved in similarly unconventional conflicts in the past. Guerrilla warfare took place during the American Civil War (1861–1865) and in the military's subsequent battles with Native Americans. It also occurred in the Philippines after the Spanish-American War (1898) and in Haiti between 1915 and 1934. Scholars have suggested the US military

UNDERGROUND FORTRESSES

One ingenious strategy used by the Communist forces in South Vietnam was the construction of underground tunnels in which they hid soldiers, weapons, and planning documents. These places provided areas from which to hide or escape from US soldiers, offered safe training facilities for Vietcong, and served as paths between key posts aboveground.

The tunnels were constructed to allow the enemy to remain concealed from US soldiers for extended periods. The hiding places boasted kitchens and sleeping areas. Many were also quite intricate. One located just 20 miles (32 km) from the South Vietnamese capital of Saigon featured 130 miles (210 km) of tunnels.[6]

Marching through thick, unfamiliar jungles left US troops extremely vulnerable to enemy fire.

THE AIR CAVALRY

The Battle of Ia Drang Valley saw the introduction of the air cavalry as a new US fighting force in Vietnam. Troops were transported by helicopters, which provided greater mobility. The air cavalry was created during the Kennedy administration to enhance the ability of the military to wage a ground war.

forgot its own history during the Vietnam War. Rather than remembering these unconventional conflicts, the military used its experience in the relatively conventional World War II to plan strategy.

US combat units in Vietnam did fight occasional large-scale battles. Among the bloodiest was in the Ia Drang Valley in November 1965, where combat between US troops and the NVA lasted two days and cost 300 US lives. The battle also resulted in 1,300 deaths for the NVA, but the discrepancy did not seem to matter.[7] It was a psychological defeat to US soldiers, and hopes for an easy victory in the war were quickly dashed. The United States began realizing that not only did the NVA have more fighting ability than expected, but there were far more of them in South Vietnam than originally believed.

As Lieutenant General Harold G. Moore wrote in the book *We Were Soldiers Once . . . And Young*:

General Westmoreland thought he had found the answer to the question of how to win this war. . . . He would trade one American life for ten or eleven or twelve North Vietnamese lives, day after day, until Ho Chi Minh cried uncle. Westmoreland would learn, too late, that he was wrong; that the American people didn't see a kill ratio of 10–1 or even 20–1 as any kind of bargain.[8]

The North Vietnamese counted on that. They planned to keep fighting until the United States lost its desire to fight.

MORE TROOPS, NO CLOSER TO VICTORY

A further 200,000 US troops arrived in Vietnam in 1966.[1] Those soldiers and the ones they joined in Vietnam won a series of combat victories over North Vietnamese forces that year. The enemy was being killed at a far greater rate than were the Americans.

Yet the Communists had gained a psychological advantage. One theory is that the North Vietnamese and Vietcong felt greater passion for and had higher personal stakes in their mission than did many US soldiers. They fought in their home country against forces dealing with unfamiliar territory thousands of miles from home. They were fighting to

The total number of US troops in Vietnam rose to more than 300,000 by the end of 1966.

unify their country in what to them was a civil war. In addition, though many South Vietnamese wanted their nation to be unified, they did not want unification under Communist control. The ruthlessness of their government played a huge role in driving others to the Vietcong.

AGENT ORANGE

US military leaders believed the unique war fought in Vietnam called for unique strategies. They needed to flush out Vietcong soldiers hiding in the dense jungles of South Vietnam, so a chemical called Agent Orange that destroyed plant life was sprayed into these areas. The substance was named for the orange stripe painted on its storage containers.

The United States began using Agent Orange early in the war. It was later discovered to cause cancer, skin rashes, and liver disease. In 1979, US veterans sued chemical companies that manufactured Agent Orange. The result was a $180 million settlement for damages.[2]

The Americans were forced to play a game of hide-and-seek. They stepped up their bombing campaign against North Vietnamese targets and tried to flush out the Vietcong in the South with air strikes. American bombers dropped chemicals on jungles in an effort to destroy Vietcong hiding places.

The US military was winning individual battles in 1966 but it was no closer to winning the war. General Westmoreland believed they could win a war of

General Westmoreland, *center*, with President Johnson, *right*, at a press conference

attrition—that the more enemy soldiers US troops could kill the closer they would be to North Vietnamese surrender. The opposite proved to be true. The Communists were winning the war of attrition. The more US troops they killed, the louder the protests from the American people and their political leaders became.

The United States indeed saw several military triumphs in 1966, driving the Vietcong away from Saigon, defeating large

STORIES FROM THE WAR

Rear Admiral Frances T. Shea Buckley served in the Nurse Corps of the US Navy and worked on a hospital ship off the coast of Vietnam in 1968. She spoke about seeing patients who had little chance of surviving their wounds:

"When patients came in and the chance of survivability was almost nil, they referred to them as GORKs, which really meant 'God only really knows.' Terrible expression. But it meant that they were so far gone that you couldn't always tell. Frequently, they would be put to the last or screened off where they could die in peace. Or if, at the end of the day, or night, they were still alive, they'd attempt them [surgeries]. In some instances, they were saved. But in some instances, death was imminent when they came on the ship."[3]

concentrations of Communist forces, and capturing enemy combatants and weapons. US troops also saw success against the NVA that year. In July, US Marines fought alongside ARVN allies in Operation Hastings, pursuing thousands of NVA troops near the border between North and South Vietnam and achieving a notable victory.

GAME OF CAT AND MOUSE

The string of US victories did not seem to matter. No matter how many NVA and Vietcong forces were killed in battle, fresh troops always appeared to take up the fight. The NVA and Vietcong were more accustomed to warfare in the jungles and mountainous terrain of Vietnam than were the Americans. North Vietnamese commander Vo Nguyen Giap explained the planning of his military:

> *When the Americans tried to apply their "seek and destroy" tactic, we responded with our own particular tactic that was to make their objective unattainable and destroy them instead. We had to. . . force the enemy to fight the way we wanted them to fight. We had to force the enemy to fight on unfamiliar territory.*[4]

The increasing number of antiwar protesters in the United States simply wanted US soldiers to return home. The outrage against US involvement in Vietnam was not simply a reaction to US battlefield deaths. Many believed the fate of a country halfway around the world should be determined by its own people. They were disturbed by the staggering number of innocent Vietnamese civilians killed by troops from both sides. They were indignant that American boys were old enough to be killed in Vietnam but were too young to vote. The voting age at the time was 21, while 18-year-olds could be drafted to fight overseas. The draft, a random selection process for adding young men to the military, sent thousands of people unwillingly to Vietnam.

A growing legion of political leaders and other influential Americans joined the ranks of protesters in 1967 as the troop count escalated and the scope of the war widened. One of the most prominent was civil rights leader Martin Luther King Jr. Some were taken aback that King, who had focused on ending discrimination against blacks in the United States, would shift his focus to speak out against the war. But he was angered that a large number of African Americans were being sent to Vietnam to fight for their country when there was still so much

Martin Luther King Jr. gave an antiwar speech to a crowd of 125,000 in New York City on April 15, 1967.

racism at home. King made his views clear in a speech given at a New York church on April 4, 1967:

> We were taking the young black men who had been crippled by our society and sending them 8,000 miles [12,900 km] away to guarantee liberties in Southeast Asia which they had not found in southwest Georgia and East Harlem.[5]

Many Americans agreed with King's sentiments. The demonstrations against the war were growing in number and intensity. Those who vowed to bring the war to the streets of the United States were about to accomplish their goal.

THE UNSEEN ENEMY

How do you fight an enemy you cannot identify? That was the question frustrated, angry US soldiers were asking in 1967. The Vietcong's intricate tunnel systems had allowed them to establish a growing presence in South Vietnam, even in a stronghold near Saigon known as the Iron Triangle. Many South Vietnamese civilians who lost faith in the government were giving aid to Vietcong fighters, and some of them even joined combat.

In 1967, US military strategists called for an extensive search-and-destroy mission known as Operation Cedar Falls to break up the Iron Triangle. It was the largest US ground operation of the war. Elaborate underground tunnels storing food and ammunition were discovered during the sweep

Soldiers nicknamed "tunnel rats" were dropped into Vietcong tunnels with pistols to clear the enemy hiding places.

of the area. US Major General William E. DePuy praised the effectiveness with which the plan was executed, calling it a "decisive turning point . . . and a blow from which the [Vietcong] in this area may never recover."[1]

But it seemed plugging one leak in Vietnam always created another. Approximately 700 Vietcong were killed in the campaign, but the huge majority fled toward the bordering country of Cambodia, where they continued to be supplied with food and weapons via the Ho Chi Minh trail.[2]

US forces were exasperated by the ability of the enemy to escape. Ordered to chase down the fleeing Vietcong, they alienated much of the civilian population by evacuating and destroying nearby villages in which they suspected the Vietcong could be hiding. US television viewers became familiar with the sight of US soldiers setting the homes of South Vietnamese villagers ablaze.

The Vietnam War was the first American war shown extensively in graphic and bloody detail back home on television. Coverage of the events gave ammunition to the antiwar movement, whose members grew increasingly angry at the growing death toll. Many were no longer content to demonstrate peacefully. They were becoming more impatient

A television news camera crew rides on a US tank in Vietnam.

for the United States to get out of Vietnam, even as the troop count was swelling to nearly 500,000 by the end of 1967.[3]

VIOLENCE IN WASHINGTON

On October 21, an estimated 35,000 protesters converged on the Pentagon in Washington, DC, the center of the US military.[4] Some showed their defiance by burning their draft cards. Approximately 2,500 US Army troops met the demonstrators.[5] One iconic image that emerged from the event was a young man placing a flower in the barrel of a bayoneted rifle held by a soldier.

The massive protest at the Pentagon was mirrored by antiwar protests at the same time in Japan and Europe.

The most vehement demonstrations against the war played out on college campuses until the Tet Offensive changed the opinions held by much of the rest of the country. The outrage among students heightened when they learned of friends or brothers having been killed in Vietnam. Millions of young men volunteered to fight or were involuntarily inducted into the military through the draft. Others in the antiwar movement or who silently opposed US involvement feared they too would be selected.

That was just what North Vietnamese leader Ho Chi Minh was counting on. The two sides were no closer to peace in 1967 than they had been before. Heavy US bombing proved ineffective in weakening North Vietnam's resolve.

Many US political leaders who had previously supported the war were becoming disenchanted. They would have preferred to stop Communism in Southeast Asia, but they came to believe the military tactics being used were not working. They concluded the strategy of General Westmoreland to overwhelm the enemy with superior firepower was failing.

A BLEAK OUTLOOK

The bleak picture might have been brightened if the United States could have won over the opinions of the South Vietnamese people. But most simply yearned to live in peace. The South Vietnamese did not feel strongly enough about the advantages of any economic or political system to have their nation torn apart over it. As the war dragged on, some South Vietnamese civilians began to see a Communist victory

WAITING AND WONDERING

All US men were required to register for the draft when they reached the age of 18. Draft calls were issued once per month, but the system was skewed against the poor. College students could receive deferments to postpone military service. Those who could not afford college, including many blacks and rural whites, were more often sent to fight. Some resisted by fleeing to Canada or accepting jail terms. Those who claimed to be conscientious objectors had to prove their moral opposition to war to avoid enlistment.

Winning the hearts and minds of the Vietnamese people
was key to progress for the United States in Vietnam.

as the only path to unification of their country, so they either
assisted or joined the Vietcong. A journalist who challenged
a US military briefing officer during a press conference raised
the issue. "It appears you [have] leveled virtually every village
and hamlet, killed or driven more than 50,000 peasants off the
land with your firepower," the reporter began. "My question is,

how do you intend to go about winning the hearts and minds of these people?" The briefing officer admitted it was a "real good question" but declined to offer a reply.[6]

There seemed to be no answers to the problems in Vietnam. After the Tet Offensive further ravaged South Vietnam in 1968, the majority of Americans wanted the troops to come home. But neither of the two men running for president—Democrat Hubert H. Humphrey and Republican Richard Nixon—were ready to take that step. One of the most tumultuous years in US history was now underway.

DISTURBING TREND

The lack of enthusiasm by US soldiers about their mission in Vietnam led to the occasional use of violence against superior officers. A few soldiers who believed their officers were too strict or were likely to send them on dangerous missions attempted to assassinate them.

This practice, which either threatened or cost the lives of several hundred US officers, was known as fragging. The word was borrowed from the name of the weapon most often used to carry out these murders—the fragmentation grenade. Sometimes, soldiers would leave the pin of a used grenade near the officer's bed as a warning. If the behavior did not change, they would throw a live grenade in, killing the officer. Instances of fragging increased as the war dragged on.

6

ATROCITIES IN VIETNAM AND BATTLES AT HOME

A platoon called Charlie Company, commanded by Lieutenant William Calley, was ordered into the tiny South Vietnamese village of My Lai on the morning of March 16, 1968. His superiors claimed civilians in the village had been aiding the Vietcong. The US soldiers were told to kill everyone because they were either Vietcong or sympathetic to the enemy.

When they arrived, they saw only innocent villagers going about their business. There was no threat of harm. But to some in Charlie Company, orders were orders. They rounded up hundreds of terrified men, women, and children and shot

A US soldier stokes the fires consuming the village of My Lai.

Calley, *left*, claimed to be following orders during the My Lai Massacre.

them to death. Only the bravery of US helicopter pilot Hugh Thompson, who told his men to shoot their fellow soldiers if they attempted to kill another civilian, prevented more bloodshed. Thompson evacuated survivors and reported the incident to his superiors.

The US Army worked to conceal the atrocity, and it was not until late in 1969 that the details leaked out. The world was horrified, but there was little retribution for the atrocity. The only target for prosecutors was Calley, who was convicted of first-degree murder and sentenced to life in prison. His superior officer was acquitted of charges. Calley's punishment was subsequently reduced to house arrest and he was free by 1974.

What became known as the My Lai Massacre prompted heated debate in the United States. Some claimed the incident was the result of a breakdown in troop discipline. Others saw it as evidence of the inhumanity of war. They claimed the military brainwashed soldiers into dehumanizing the enemy to make it easier to kill them.

The North Vietnamese and Vietcong forces had been responsible for many more horrific large-scale atrocities. During the Tet Offensive, thousands of civilians and prisoners of war were

THE STORY OF KIM PHUC

Perhaps the most heart-wrenching photograph to emerge from the war showed 9-year-old Kim Phuc fleeing from her village and screaming in pain. She had been a victim of napalm, a gasoline mixture dropped by US and South Vietnamese aircraft to scorch jungles and villages. It burned people to the bone with temperatures of 5,000 degrees Fahrenheit (2,760°C).[1]

News photographer Nick Ut captured her terror. He also heroically poured water on her wounds and rushed her to the hospital. She later moved to Toronto, Canada, and established the Kim Phuc Foundation, which provides medical and psychological assistance to child victims of war.

slaughtered in the city of Hue. But the media focused largely on the My Lai Massacre, helping to sway public opinion further against the war.

TRAGEDIES BACK IN THE UNITED STATES

The mass murder at My Lai was followed by two murders in the United States that threatened to tear apart the country. The assassination of civil rights leader Martin Luther King Jr. on April 4, 1968, prompted rioting among inner city blacks that cost more lives. Two months later, presidential candidate Robert F. Kennedy was shot and killed. The brother of slain president John F. Kennedy was on the verge of clinching the Democratic nomination and was a favorite to win the presidency on a platform to end US involvement in the war.

The loss of Kennedy destroyed any hope by the antiwar movement that US troops would be withdrawn. His murder left Democrat Hubert Humphrey and Republican Richard Nixon to run for the White House. Both favored maintaining US forces in Vietnam and attempting to achieve what Nixon called "peace with honor."[2]

Anger reached a boiling point in late August during the Democratic National Convention in Chicago, Illinois. There it

Protesters confront police officers during the 1968 Democratic National Convention.

was confirmed the war policy of President Johnson would be continued. Thousands of furious antiwar protesters converged on the city. Many were unafraid to use violence to show their rage. Mayor Richard Daley was equally intent in fighting fire with fire. His law enforcement officials attacked demonstrators in what has been described as a police riot.

Millions of Americans watched on television as more than 18,000 Chicago police and national guardsmen rushed

FINAL PLEA FROM HO CHI MINH

North Vietnamese leader Ho Chi Minh died of a heart attack on September 3, 1969, and was replaced by Communist Party head Le Duan. Minh sought to buoy the spirits of his people and his troops, even in death. In his will, he urged them to fight until every US soldier was out of Vietnam.

into the crowd.[3] They beat protesters, journalists, and even innocent bystanders with clubs. Hundreds of often bloodied antiwar demonstrators were pushed into police vans to be arrested.

TALKING PEACE

The United States and North Vietnam finally began negotiating for peace in Paris in May 1968, but their efforts went nowhere. The United States demanded the NVA leave South Vietnam. The North Vietnamese sought Communist representation in a postwar South Vietnamese government. Neither side would consider the other's proposals.

In one of his last acts as president, Johnson halted Operation Rolling Thunder, the bombing of North Vietnam. The attempt to lure North Vietnam back to the bargaining table failed. But the number of US forces in South Vietnam began decreasing for the first time. In November, Nixon won the presidential election. When he was sworn into office, the troop level peaked at approximately 540,000.[4] Nixon announced a plan called Vietnamization in which US soldiers would be slowly pulled out of Vietnam and replaced by ARVN forces over the next few years.

The pace of the withdrawal did not satisfy activists in the antiwar movement, who were angered when the US death toll in 1968 was the highest yearly total since the war began: 16,899.[5] Antiwar activists became more horrified in May, when a bloody struggle in the A Shau Valley of South Vietnam resulted in 142 US deaths and 731 wounded.[6]

The war was changing in many ways. Some US soldiers were becoming more interested in simply staying alive rather than risking their lives to win the war. Often-unprepared South Vietnamese troops were trained to take over the fighting. The enemy was gaining strength and gaining ground. US antiwar demonstrations were growing in size and intensity. Finally, the end of the war was coming into view. But it was not the kind of end about which US generals had been optimistic.

The battle of Hamburger Hill received its name for the way it "ground up" so many men. The battle began on May 10, 1969, when US troops began fighting to capture a hill known as Dong Ap Bia, also called Hill 937. They knew it was going to be a dangerous mission when they were told to pack twice the usual ammunition. The hill was being used by the NVA as a hub for transporting men and weapons to the coastal area around Hue, a city that had been a target of enemy forces during the Tet Offensive. Repeated attempts to take the hill were repelled.

US soldier Arthur Wiknik described the terror he felt after the assault began. "It was just mayhem," he said. "You could hear the bullets coming in. . . . As long as they didn't hit you, you know you were safe, but you had to get away from that spot because you were being targeted. You were so close to your life ending, there was another sense taking over."[7]

The Americans finally captured Dong Ap Bia but withdrew less than a month later. Military leaders claimed the need to secure the hill had been eliminated since the enemy had been driven from the area. But those who fought the battle believed many had died for nothing. Even President Nixon questioned

US troops fight their way up Hamburger Hill.

the point of the operation. He launched a policy that would end search-and-destroy tactics and place Americans in a more defensive posture in an attempt to limit their casualties.

WITHDRAWAL AND EXPANSION

B y 1969, President Nixon was faced with what seemed like an impossible task in Vietnam. He was trying to prevent a Communist takeover in South Vietnam while keeping US troops out of harm's way. He was attempting to bomb the North Vietnamese into submission, but that merely strengthened their resolve. He was trying to turn the job of fighting the war over to the South Vietnamese forces, but they were unable to stave off the enemy. He hoped US soldiers would maintain strong morale, but many simply wanted to return home alive.

Nixon repeated his desire to achieve "peace with honor" throughout the early years of his presidency. He turned to

Nixon gave a televised address discussing his Vietnamization program.

National Security Advisor Henry Kissinger, who met with North Vietnamese diplomat Xuan Thuy in 1969 without success.

Americans on both sides of the political fence grew more vehement about their stands. Pro-war officials called for air strikes against both military and civilian targets in North Vietnam. Nixon decided against that tactic, which might have drawn China into the conflict. Antiwar advocates took to the streets in greater numbers in 1969 than ever before. The movement had exploded far beyond college campuses, and millions of citizens were now participating in protests and demonstrations all over the country.

On October 15, 1969, the antiwar movement peaked. The first Moratorium Day was staged to protest continued US involvement in Vietnam. In towns big and small throughout the nation, church bells tolled. Marchers holding hands bellowed out the names of slain US soldiers. Students orchestrated walkouts from school. Protesters held similar demonstrations in Australia, France, and the United Kingdom. Even US soldiers on patrol in Vietnam displayed their antiwar solidarity by wearing black armbands.

Moratorium Day protesters massed in the nation's capital.

UNWAVERING PRESIDENT

Another moratorium was held exactly one month later. Approximately 500,000 demonstrators converged on Washington, DC, to protest the war.[1] Yet Nixon remained steadfast. He claimed the United States would lose respect around the world if it pulled its troops out of Vietnam, or if the United States lost the war.

Military officials complained in early 1970 that the NVA and Vietcong were using the bordering country of Cambodia

71

to escape from US forces and stock up on weapons and ammunition. So on April 30, Nixon told a national television audience he was dispatching troops into Cambodia. Millions perceived the strategy as an expansion of a war they desperately wanted to end. The antiwar movement, which had finally quieted on college campuses, exploded into violence.

Kent State University in northeast Ohio had not been a hotbed of student activism. But the news of the invasion of Cambodia prompted its students to burn down the Reserve Officers' Training Corps building on May 2. Continued demonstrations motivated Ohio governor James Rhodes to send in the National Guard, which failed to quell the protests. Rhodes, who backed US policy in Vietnam, criticized the protesters, calling them "the worst type of people that we harbor in America." He added: "We are going to eradicate the problem. We are not going to treat the symptoms."[2]

Tension mounted on May 4. Some protesters began throwing rocks at the guardsmen. Others threw back tear gas canisters the guardsmen had thrown at them. In response, some of the guardsmen shot into the crowd, killing four students. Two were not involved in the protests and were just walking between classes.

A bystander kneels over the body of Jeffrey Miller, shot by a National Guardsman at Kent State University.

College campuses throughout the country erupted into violence, forcing many to shut down. And on May 15, police killed two more students at Jackson State University in Mississippi during an antiwar protest.

STORIES FROM THE WAR

Lou Cusella was the roommate of Bill Schroeder, who was killed in the Kent State shootings. Cusella spoke about heightening tensions at Kent State:

"The governor's confrontational rhetoric of May 3 escalated the tension. After the Guard swept through the campus on the evening of May 3 the time was ripe for a cathartic reaction on May 4. The mood on the campus on May 4 was mystical; I can't explain it but it was a highly dramatic event. The Guard were invaders. . . . I really look at the incident as an example of how authorities often resort to lethal force to prove their credibility. The students were armed with words and symbols, and maybe even a few rocks. There is no reason for the guard's action."[3]

THE CAMBODIA MISSION

The protests were too late to stop the combined force of 15,000 US and South Vietnamese troops who had crossed the Cambodian border following Nixon's speech. They destroyed huge stockpiles of weapons and ammunition found at a base camp. They reported 11,349 Communist soldiers killed.[4] But the NVA soon regained control of eastern Cambodia. The mission also showed the ARVN was far too dependent on US air support and were no match for a strong and confident enemy.

The action motivated the war-weary US Congress to ban US forces from operating outside of South Vietnam, and the political backlash against the war gained momentum. The Senate

A SURPRISE VISITOR

It was 4:00 a.m. on May 10, 1970. A few students who had participated in an antiwar protest were hanging around the Lincoln Memorial in Washington, DC. They could hardly believe their eyes when President Nixon's car pulled up.

Nixon had been restless. Distressed by the killings at Kent State six days earlier and the violent reactions on college campuses, he decided to make an impromptu visit to the memorial when he came upon the students. One student from the Syracuse University expressed shock that Nixon talked to him not about the war, but about that school's football team.

overwhelmingly voted to rescind the Gulf of Tonkin Resolution, which had allowed the president to take whatever steps he deemed necessary to halt Communist aggression in Vietnam.

General Creighton Abrams, who had replaced William Westmoreland as the commander of US forces in Vietnam months after the Tet Offensive, changed the US military strategy. Rather than treating the war as a conventional war, Abrams began using counterinsurgency tactics. He split large groups of soldiers into smaller units with more focused goals, and put a larger emphasis on training the South Vietnamese armed forces. The new strategy began showing positive results, but by this time the war had already been lost politically at home.

The North Vietnamese understood the United States was in a tenuous position. The withdrawal of Americans continued, as did the training of South Vietnamese troops to take over the fighting. However, the Vietnamization program was not transforming the ARVN into an effective force. The South Vietnamese were provided with the most modern US weaponry and accompanied their United States allies on missions. Still, they remained ineffective. The NVA strategy was to bide its time until the US soldiers were gone.

A US helicopter is loaded with equipment during the military's withdrawal from Cambodia.

Their first major test for the ARVN was an attack into neighboring Laos, which was suspected of supplying and sheltering the enemy. A force of 21,000 ARVN troops set up bases in that country but faltered in the face of Communist fire. NVA forces chased them back toward the South Vietnamese border, and an estimated 10,000 were killed, wounded, or captured.[5] Only air support from US helicopters prevented even heavier losses. The war effort appeared doomed to failure, and US troop morale hit an all-time low. And some who returned home from Vietnam brought their anger and hatred of the war with them.

COMING HOME

B efore Vietnam, US veterans of foreign wars had always returned home to heroes' welcomes. This situation would change for veterans of the Vietnam War. Some Americans felt indignation over their nation's involvement in the war, believing it was morally wrong to contribute as a soldier to a conflict that had resulted in the deaths of so many people. Many of them did not consider that a large number of veterans did not volunteer to fight and were instead drafted. Some antiwar activists treated soldiers who had fought in Vietnam with contempt.

Most veterans were proud of their service and angry over the treatment by those who disrespected them. But some agreed with protesters who believed the war was a tragic waste of life. They disagreed that the fall of South Vietnam to Communism would inevitably lead to the fall of other nations

Soldiers' families were happy to see them return home, but some antiwar activists treated Vietnam veterans disrespectfully.

in Southeast Asia. They felt US political leaders had deceived them into believing they were fighting for freedom.

Among the veterans who had grown disenchanted with the war was future US senator and secretary of state John Kerry. He tossed his war decorations over a fence at the US Capitol building as part of a Vietnam Veterans Against the War protest in Washington, DC. He also addressed the Senate Committee on Foreign Affairs in April 1971. He spoke philosophically about what he felt was a misdirected cause. "How do you ask a man to be the last man to die in Vietnam?" he said. "How do you ask a man to be the last man to die for a mistake?"[1]

President Nixon was not ready to admit the mistake. He maintained the policy of withdrawing US troops while training the South Vietnamese to hold off a Communist takeover. But the ARVN was not keeping the NVA back. The North Vietnamese attacked the provincial capital of Quang Tri City in the spring of 1972, and the ARVN quickly retreated. By mid-April, the threat of a South Vietnamese collapse appeared quite real.

Veteran John Kerry, wounded three times in Vietnam, spoke out strongly against the war.

RELIEVING SOUTH VIETNAM

Because Congress would not have allowed Nixon to redeploy US ground troops, the president believed air strikes against North Vietnamese strongholds in South Vietnam were the only solution. He dispatched US warships, aircraft carriers, and warplanes to bomb enemy supply lines in what became known as Operation Linebacker. They also delivered equipment to

THE PENTAGON PAPERS

Among the most controversial incidents of the Vietnam War era revolved around US Department of Defense analyst Daniel Ellsburg. Ellsburg sought to provide the *New York Times* with documents detailing the department's secret history and analysis of the war. What became known as the Pentagon Papers proved that President Johnson lied to the public about the military progress being made in Vietnam. The Nixon administration failed to prevent the *Times* from publishing the damaging documents in 1971. The Supreme Court ruled the newspaper had a legal right to print them. Though the government attempted to take legal action against Ellsburg, the charges were dismissed.

the ARVN. At the same time, Nixon ordered new air strikes against North Vietnam itself, which continued for the duration of the war.

The strategy temporarily prevented the NVA from receiving enough supplies to achieve victory and unify Vietnam under the Communist flag. But Nixon and national security head Henry Kissinger understood a takeover was only a matter of time unless they negotiated a peace settlement that maintained a US-friendly government in South Vietnam. Since North Vietnam felt it was on the verge of achieving its military goals, this negotiation would require a creative approach.

Nixon's visit to China was the first-ever visit by a US president since China had become Communist in 1949.

Nixon took the surprising step of visiting the two most powerful Communist countries in the world: China and the Soviet Union. Both had supported North Vietnam. Though his official mission was to improve relations with those two nations, it has been speculated the trips were intended to frighten the North Vietnamese into believing he could convince them to cut off military support. That theory might never be proven, but North Vietnam did return to peace talks with the United States in 1972.

Previous efforts had proven fruitless. But it appeared discussions between Kissinger and North Vietnamese negotiator Le Duc Tho had culminated in an agreement as the 1972 presidential election approached. US troops would withdraw and US prisoners of war would be returned. The agreement also called for free elections in South Vietnam. But the United States withdrew its demand that North Vietnam pull its military out of South Vietnam. Despite objections from the South Vietnamese

FROM PRISONER TO PRESIDENTIAL CANDIDATE

A Russian-made missile shot down US pilot John McCain over North Vietnam on October 26, 1967. His plane landed in a lake. He had broken his right leg and both arms. But that was the least of his problems. He would spend nearly six years as a prisoner of war in North Vietnam.

McCain was tortured and told he would never go home again. He was finally released with other US prisoners of war in 1973 and embarked on a career in politics. He became a Republican US senator and later lost the 2008 presidential election to Barack Obama.

government, Kissinger proclaimed in late October that peace had been achieved.

EASY WIN FOR NIXON

It was perfect timing for Nixon. The news clinched a lopsided victory over Democrat George McGovern in the 1972 presidential election, giving Nixon a second term in office. But the announcement proved premature. American negotiators again requested the North Vietnamese leave South Vietnam. Tho refused and the conflict resumed. Nixon responded with the heaviest air strikes of the war. He ordered more than 20,000 short tons (18,100 metric tons) of bombs dropped on Hanoi, the capital of North Vietnam, and Haiphong.[2]

The North Vietnamese returned to the bargaining table by the end of 1972. Americans and their political leaders had made it clear they were fed up with the war, which made Nixon and Kissinger desperate for a deal. They took back their request for the NVA to withdraw from South Vietnam, asking only for the right to continue giving aid to that country. The result was a peace treaty signed by the United States, North Vietnam, South Vietnam, and the Vietcong on January 27, 1973. Nixon told the American people peace with honor had been achieved. He also

A surprise North Vietnamese attack on South Vietnam launched on March 30, 1972, was known as the Easter Offensive. It rocked the unprepared ARVN, which could no longer depend on widespread protection from US ground forces.

The South Vietnamese relied on one of the most extensive US aerial assaults in history. President Nixon ordered a massive bombing of key North Vietnamese targets in a mission known as Operation Linebacker, which began on April 6. The Seventh Air Force carried out the battering from the sky against North Vietnamese targets. Fires caused by the bombing of fuel storage tanks could be seen from 110 miles (180 km) away.

When the earliest attacks failed to slow the NVA offensive, Nixon called for mining of Haiphong Harbor and bombing of North Vietnamese airfields, power plants, and other targets. Air strikes also disrupted the flow of weapons and other supplies to the Vietcong in the South.

Operation Linebacker eventually halted the NVA advance. Along with visits from President Nixon to China and the Soviet

The North Vietnamese air defenses shot down 27 US aircraft during Linebacker II, killing 43 crew members.

Union, the bombing helped lure North Vietnamese leaders into peace negotiations with the United States.

When a deal struck in late October 1972 failed to keep the peace, Nixon ordered a massive bombing attack against Hanoi and Haiphong known as Operation Linebacker II, which was credited for leading to the peace treaty of January 1973. But Nixon ordered more air strikes against Hanoi when it became obvious North Vietnam planned on continuing military operations until South Vietnam was overrun.

President Nixon, *right*, met with President Thieu of South Vietnam, *left*, in California in April 1973.

reassured the South Vietnamese that they controlled their own destiny. "By your courage, by your sacrifice, you have won the precious right to determine your own future and you have developed the strength to defend that right," he said. "We look forward to working with you in the future, friends in peace as we have been allies in war."[3]

The agreement stated all military action must cease in South Vietnam. The nation's government was to be divided into two factions, one led by South Vietnamese president Nguyen Van Thieu and another controlled by the Communists. The treaty also stipulated a unified Vietnam must come about peacefully.

That did not happen. Nixon distrusted the North Vietnamese. He vowed to Thieu the US would respond militarily if the NVA and Vietcong continued fighting. The president ordered bombing of enemy supply routes in Cambodia, but there was no chance of Nixon sending in ground troops. Congress made sure of that by passing the War Powers Act, which mandated congressional approval before a president could send troops into battle.

THE WAR IS LOST

The Paris Peace Accords were signed on January 27, 1973, but all sides involved in the Vietnam War viewed them largely as worthless scraps of paper. Maintaining the peace was turned over to the International Commission of Control and Supervision (ICCS). Representatives of the ICCS from Poland, Hungary, Canada, and Indonesia had been instructed to oversee the cease-fire. Yet the guns and artillery still blasted away.

The last US troops left the country on March 29, but fighting between the ARVN and Communist forces continued throughout South Vietnam. Accusations of breaking the cease-fire came from both sides. The treaty did not distinguish territorial boundaries between the warring parties. Battles had raged immediately before the cease-fire as both sides sought to seize as much territory as possible. The ARVN was positioned in heavily populated areas, which allowed

US diplomat Henry Kissinger, *lower left*, helped negotiate the Paris Peace Accords on behalf of the United States.

Communist troops to overrun hundreds of villages and control supply routes surrounding the South Vietnamese capital of Saigon. The ARVN recaptured nearly all of the villages before the cease-fire took effect.

Still, Communist forces proved more active after the cease-fire than before. Their military increased in size and scope over the previous year, and they worked to strengthen the Vietcong. By late October, US officials were complaining the North Vietnamese had transported 70,000 men, 400 tanks and 200 pieces of artillery into the south since the cease-fire. By the middle of 1973, they boasted a force of 176,000 in South Vietnam.[1]

President Nixon made secret commitments to continue aiding South Vietnam. But in November 1973, a vote in Congress made certain he could not fulfill his promise to Thieu to provide military aid if North Vietnam threatened a takeover. Congress required Nixon to notify it at least two days in advance of planned troop deployment for approval. It further stipulated congressional approval for any forces remaining in Vietnam longer than two months.

Even after US forces left the country, the South Vietnamese military continued the fight.

LAST STAND FOR THE ARVN

A desperate Thieu inflicted heavy NVA losses by ordering surprise attacks against Communist targets. But the North Vietnamese launched a counterattack in the spring of 1974, regaining all the territory they had lost and then some. The NVA seized the initiative and never lost it, striking again in December and capturing the South Vietnamese city of Ban Me Thuot in early March 1975. The ARVN retreated while civilians fled, resulting in disorder and confusion.

The North Vietnamese felt they were on the verge of winning the war and they pounced on the opportunity. They captured the provincial capital of Hue and the key city of Da Nang. They were steamrolling to the capital city of Saigon, where Thieu resigned on April 21 and blamed the United States for the impending collapse of his government. "The United States has not respected its promises," he said. "It is inhumane. It is untrustworthy. It is irresponsible."[2]

The final NVA push began on April 29, 1975. The remaining Americans in Saigon were hurriedly evacuated in Operation Frequent Wind, but thousands of South Vietnamese yearned to follow them out of the country. An estimated 6,000 were stuffed into helicopters and 22,000 others were picked up by navy warships.[3] Some were children dropped off by parents who knew they were parting with them forever. Thousands of other South Vietnamese fled in their own boats.

Temporary South Vietnamese leader Duong Van Minh announced the surrender of his country to North Vietnamese forces the next day. The NVA captured Saigon and renamed it Ho Chi Minh City. The unification of Vietnam under Communist rule was complete.

American sailors pushed helicopters off their ships to make more room for South Vietnamese evacuees.

AFTERMATH OF WAR

Vietnam went through a transformation after unification. People who supported South Vietnam during the war were sent to reeducation camps. But though the country remained officially Communist, it embraced social and economic changes in the 1980s that improved the lives of its citizens. Vietnam has since reestablished diplomatic relations with the United States.

Meanwhile, the US antiwar faction and those who supported US policy continue arguing their points, but debates have become less heated with time. There can be little doubt,

The Vietnam Veterans Memorial Wall was designed by
21-year-old architecture student Maya Lin.

however, that the Vietnam War changed the country forever
and in a profound way. Members of the American public have
become far more likely to question their government, especially
when the government seeks to send troops to fight on foreign

soil. They have grown more skeptical of their political leaders in general.

Americans have also become more sympathetic to the plight of the veterans returning from war. The moral outrage felt by many during the conflict spilled over into a hatred of soldiers who fought in Vietnam. Most now agree their anger was misplaced. Many concluded that those who serve in the military, especially during wartime, deserve respect and understanding upon returning home. The Vietnam Veterans Memorial opened in Washington, DC, in 1982. Its centerpiece is a large, V-shaped slab of rock etched with the names of all the members of the military killed or missing in action in Southeast Asia.

The Vietnam War divided the nation. But it was also a learning experience for those who lived through it. The lessons gained from the war have proven useful to generations who followed. Other wars in which the United States has engaged, such as the invasion of Iraq in 2003, have also prompted debate. But none of the recent debates have motivated more passionate exchanges than those that raged during the Vietnam War.

1954

Vietnam gains its independence and is split into North and South by the Geneva Accords, passed on July 21.

1957

South Vietnam president Ngo Dinh Diem speaks to the US Congress on May 9 about democracy and freedom in his country.

1961

In December, helicopter units become the first Americans involved in combat operations in Vietnam.

1964

In August, incidents involving North Vietnamese patrol boats and US ships result in passage of the Gulf of Tonkin Resolution, which grants power to President Johnson to wage an undeclared war in Vietnam.

1965

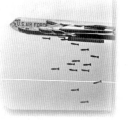

Operation Rolling Thunder, a heavy bombing campaign against North Vietnamese targets, begins in March.

1967

Antiwar demonstrations at the Pentagon in Washington, DC, from October 21 to 23 draw an estimated 35,000 protesters.

1968

The Tet Offensive begins on January 31, swaying US public opinion against the war.

1969

On April 30, President Nixon announces a Vietnamization program that will eventually turn the fighting over to the South Vietnamese.

1970

On May 4, a protest over an incursion into Cambodia announced by Nixon results in four students being shot at Kent State University in Ohio.

1973

The Paris Peace Accords are signed on January 27. The last US combat troops return home two months later.

1975

On April 30, the last Americans evacuate Saigon. North Vietnam completes its takeover of South Vietnam.

VIETNAM WAR BATTLES, 1954–1975

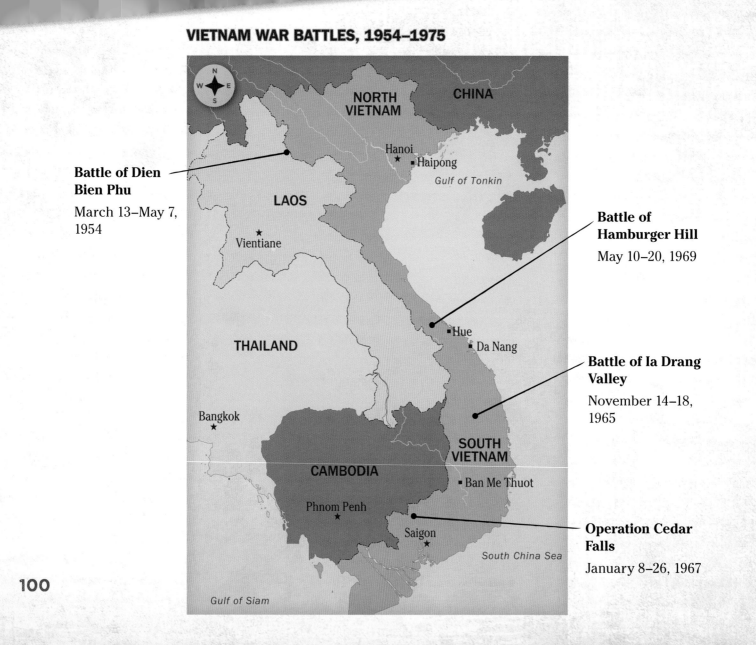

Battle of Dien Bien Phu

March 13–May 7, 1954

Battle of Hamburger Hill

May 10–20, 1969

Battle of Ia Drang Valley

November 14–18, 1965

Operation Cedar Falls

January 8–26, 1967

CASUALTIES

Total American Casualties: 361,864

- Army deaths: 38,224
- Navy deaths: 2,566
- Marines deaths: 14,844
- Air Force deaths: 2,586
- Army wounded: 201,525
- Navy wounded: 10,076
- Marines wounded: 88,594
- Air Force wounded: 3,449

KEY PLAYERS

Ho Chi Minh was the president of North Vietnam from 1945 until his death in 1969. Before the Vietnam War he had been an advocate for Vietnam's independence and unification.

Lyndon B. Johnson was the president of the United States from 1963 until 1969. He inherited a small-scale war in Vietnam from previous president John F. Kennedy, then expanded the war dramatically.

Ngo Dinh Diem was the president of South Vietnam 1955 until his death in 1963. His brutal rule and ruthless persecutions led to his removal from office and execution by his own military.

Richard M. Nixon was the president of the United States from 1969 until 1974. He pushed for Vietnamization as a way for the United States to exit the Vietnam War.

Army of the Republic of Vietnam (ARVN)

The South Vietnamese army that fought alongside the United States and against the NVA and Vietcong during the war.

base

A protected, centralized location from which military operations are planned.

Buddhist

A person who practices the religion of Buddhism.

capitalism

An economic system in which the means of production are privately owned and governed by the principles of a free-market economy: supply and demand.

democracy

A form of government that calls for free elections and liberties such as freedom of speech or freedom of the press.

demonstration

A gathering of people who come together to express their views on a particular issue or cause.

draft

The process by which American men were selected and legally bound to fight in Vietnam.

military advisers
> Noncombat US personnel who trained the South Vietnamese military before, during, and after US involvement in the Vietnam War.

North Vietnamese Army (NVA)
> The army of North Vietnam that fought alongside the Vietcong and against the United States and the ARVN in the war.

offensive
> A major military attack carried out by a large number of soldiers for the purpose of capturing territory.

overthrow
> The usually violent act of taking power by ousting those in power in a particular country.

poll
> A sampling of opinions on a subject taken from a group of people to provide an idea of overall public opinion on a particular subject.

veteran
> Any soldier who has returned from fighting in a war.

SELECTED BIBLIOGRAPHY

Moore, Lt. Gen. Harold G. and Galloway, Joseph L. *We Were Soldiers Once . . . And Young.* New York: Random, 2004. Print.

Tucker, Spencer C. *Vietnam.* Lexington, KY: The UP of Kentucky, 1999. Print.

FURTHER READINGS

Caputo, Philip. *10,000 Days of Thunder: A History of the Vietnam War.* New York: Athenium Books for Young Readers, 2005. Print.

Gitlin, Martin. *U.S. Involvement in Vietnam.* Minneapolis, MN: ABDO, 2010. Print.

WEB SITES

To learn more about the Vietnam War, visit ABDO Publishing Company online at **www.abdopublishing.com**. Web sites about the Vietnam War are featured on our Book Links page. These links are routinely monitored and updated to provide the most current information available.

PLACES TO VISIT

National Vietnam War Museum

3400 North Tanner Road
Orlando, FL 32826
407-601-2864
http://www.nwmvocf.org
The Vietnam Veterans of Central Florida donated many of the artifacts from the war that can be seen at this museum.

The Vietnam Center and Archive, Texas Tech University

2805 Fifteenth Street
Lubbock, TX 79409
806-742-9010
http://www.vietnam.ttu.edu
This center boasts a large collection of information and documentary records of the Vietnam War.

Vietnam Veterans Memorial

5 Henry Bacon Dr. NW
Washington, DC 20024
http://www.nps.gov/vive/index.htm
The names of more than 58,000 Americans killed in Vietnam are listed on this V-shaped wall.

CHAPTER 1. SURPRISE ATTACK

1. Anthony O. Edmonds. *The War in Vietnam*. Westport, CT: Greenwood, 1998. Print. 59.

2. Paul Wedel. "1968 Tet Offensive Marked Turning Point in US Loss in Vietnam." *Los Angeles Times*. Los Angeles Times, 31 Jan. 1988. Web. 11 Dec. 2012.

3. David T. Zabecki. "Tet Offensive: Overall Strategy." *Encyclopedia of the Vietnam War: Volume Two*. Santa Barbara, CA: ABC-CLIP, 1998. Print. 680.

4. Ian Stewart. "Tet-A-Tet On War New World, Lingering Memories Since The Pivotal Battle Of Vietnam." *Spokesman-Review*. Spokesman-Review, 30 Jan. 1998. Web. 4 Apr. 2013.

5. Martin Luther King Jr. "Beyond Vietnam: A Time to Break Silence." *Common Dreams*. Common Dreams.org, 15 Jan. 2004. Web. 4 Apr. 2013.

6. Spencer C. Tucker. *Vietnam*. Lexington, KY: UP of Kentucky, 1999. Print. 136.

7. "The Vietniks: Self-Defeating Dissent." *Time*. Time, 29 Oct. 1965. Web. 4 Apr. 2013.

8. Chris Matthews. "And That's the Way It Was." *New York Times*. New York Times, 6 July 2013. Web. 11 Dec. 2012.

CHAPTER 2. THE ORIGINS OF THE WAR

1. "US Death Toll from Korean War Revised Downward, Time Reports." *CNN*. CNN, 4 June 2000. Web. 3 Apr. 2013.

2. "Diem on Democracy." *New York Times*. New York Times, 12 May 1957.

3. Jeremy T. Gunn. *Spiritual Weapons: The Cold War and the Forging of an American National Religion*. Westport, CT: Greenwood, 2009. Print. 178.

CHAPTER 3. GIVING THE GREEN LIGHT

1. "Vietnam War." *Encyclopaedia Britannica*. Encyclopaedia Britannica, 2013. Web. 4 Apr. 2013.

2. Robert S. McNamara. *Argument Without End: In Search of Answers to the Vietnam Tragedy*. New York: Perseus, 1999. Print. 271.

3. "Vietnam War Allied Troop Levels." *American War Library*. American War Library, 6 Dec. 2008. Web. 4 Apr. 2013.

4. Philip Caputo. *A Rumor of War*. New York: Holt, 1977. Print. XIV.

5. "Chronology of Events." *Encyclopedia of the Vietnam War*. Santa Barbara, CA: ABC-CLIO, 1998. Print. 859.

6. "How Army Engineers Cleared Viet Cong Tunnels." *US Army Corps of Engineers*. US Army Corps of Engineers, Jan. 2003. Web. 4 Apr. 2013.

7. Blaine T. Brown and Robert C. Cottrell. *Lives and Times: Individuals and Issues in American History Since 1865*. Lanham, MD: Rowman and Littlefield, 2009. Print. 240.

8. Lt. Gen. Harold G. Moore and Joseph L. Galloway. *We Were Soldiers Once . . . And Young*. New York: Random, 1992. Print. 345.

CHAPTER 4. MORE TROOPS, NO CLOSER TO VICTORY

1. "Vietnam War Allied Troop Levels." *American War Library*. American War Library, 6 Dec. 2008. Web. 4 Apr. 2013.

2. Ralph Blumenthal. "Veterans Accept $180 Million Pact on Agent Orange." *New York Times*. New York Times, 8 May 1984. Web. 17 May 2013.

3. "Oral History Project: Interview with Frances Shea Buckley." *The Vietnam Archive*. Texas Tech University, 8 August 2005. Web. 4 Apr. 2013.

4. "Interview with Vo Nguyen Giap." *People's Century: Guerrilla Wars*. PBS, n.d. Web. 4 Apr. 2013.

5. "Declaration of Independence from the War in Vietnam." *Vietnam in America: A Documented History*. New York: Grove, 1995. Print. 311.

CHAPTER 5. THE UNSEEN ENEMY

1. John F. Votaw. "Cedar Falls, Operation." *Encyclopedia of the Vietnam War*. Santa Barbara, CA: ABC-CLIO, 1998. Print. 108.

2. Tony Jaques. *Dictionary of Battles and Sieges*. Westport, CT: Greenwood, 2007. Print. 475.

3. "Vietnam War Allied Troop Levels." *American War Library*. American War Library, 6 Dec. 2008. Web. 4 Apr. 2013.

4. "US Marshals and the Pentagon Riot of October 21, 1967." *US Marshals Service*. US Marshals Service, n.d. Web. 4 Apr. 2013.

5. Jeff Leen. "The Vietnam Protests: When Worlds Collided." *Washington Post*. Washington Post, 27 Sept. 1999. Web. 4 Apr. 2013.

6. Clark Dougan, and Stephen Weiss. *The American Experience in Vietnam*. Boston: Boston Publishing, 1988. Print. 114–115.

CHAPTER 6. ATROCITIES IN VIETNAM AND BATTLES AT HOME

1. Michael Taylor. "Military Says Goodbye to Napalm." *SF Gate*. San Francisco Chronicle, 4 Apr. 2001. Web. 4 Apr. 2013.

2. *Critical Perspectives on the Vietnam War*. Gilbert Morales, ed. New York: Rosen, 2004. Print. 123.

3. "Brief History of Chicago's 1968 Democratic Convention." *CNN*. CNN, 1997. Web. 4 Apr. 2013.

4. "Richard Nixon - America's 37th President." *Richard Nixon Foundation*. Richard Nixon Foundation, 2012. Web. 4 Apr. 2013.

5. "Statistical Information about Fatal Casualties of the Vietnam War." *National Archives*. National Archives, Oct. 2012. Web. 4 Apr. 2013.

6. "1968: The Definitive Year." *eHistory Archive*. Ohio State University, 2013. Web. 4 Apr. 2013.

7. "A Soldier's Story: Hamburger Hill." *Vietnam in HD*. History Channel, 2013. Web. 4 Apr. 2013.

CHAPTER 7. WITHDRAWAL AND EXPANSION

1. "Second Moratorium Against the War Held." *This Day in History.* History Channel, 2013. Web. 5 Apr. 2013.

2. Rick Hampson. "1970 Kent State Shootings Are an Enduring History Lesson." *USA Today.* USA Today, 4 May 2010. Web. 5 Apr. 2013.

3. "The Survivors." *May 4 Archive.* May 4 Archive, n.d. Web. 5 Apr. 2013.

4. Spencer C. Tucker. *Vietnam.* Lexington, KY: The UP of Kentucky, 1999. Print. 119.

5. Cecil B. Currey. *Victory at Any Cost.* Dulles, VA: Dulles Books, 1997. Print. 282.

CHAPTER 8. COMING HOME

1. "Vietnam War Veteran John Kerry's Testimony Before the Senate Foreign Relations Committee." *The War at Home: The Antiwar Movement.* University of Richmond, n.d. Web. 5 Apr. 2013.

2. A. J. Langguth. *Our Vietnam: The War 1954–1975.* New York: Simon, 2000. Print. 614.

3. "1973: Nixon Announces Vietnam Peace Deal." *BBC.* BBC, 2008. Web. 5 Apr. 2013.

CHAPTER 9. THE WAR IS LOST

1. Spencer C. Tucker. *Vietnam.* Lexington, KY: The UP of Kentucky, 1999. Print. 179.

2. Malcolm W. Browne. "Thieu Resigns, Calls US Untrustworthy." *New York Times* 22 Apr. 1975: A1. Print.

3. John W. Finney. "US Rescue Fleet Is Picking Up Vietnamese Who Fled in Boats." *New York Times.* New York Times, 1 May 1975. Web. 5 Apr. 2013.

ABOUT THE AUTHOR

Marty Gitlin is a freelance writer based in Cleveland, Ohio. He has written more than 70 nonfiction educational books for middle school, high school, and college students. He has won more than 45 awards during his 30 years as a writer, including first place for general excellence from the Associated Press. That organization also named him as one of the top four feature writers in Ohio.